SUPER

ENGLISH

by John McClelland and Henderson Editors
Illustrated by Peter Rutherford

HENDERSON
PUBLISHING PLC
©1995 HENDERSON PUBLISHING PLC

ENGLISH RULES, O.K.?

English is, unfortunately for you, a core subject, which means that like the plague, bedtime, Sunday afternoons and falling off your bicycle, it can't be avoided...

So what? you might think - English is English, everybody speaks it; must be better than other dopey subjects like History or Science, and ten thousand times easier than Mathematics... Wrong!

Teachers like to make things as complicated as possible. Otherwise, people might get the idea that teaching is easy and pay them less money. They have invented a whole set of stupid rules designed to make learning English just as hard as juggling six oranges whilst singing the latest Number One and swimming underwater in a whirlpool - all at the same time, of course.

This is where your survival guide will help: when you have read it, you will actually know less about English than when you started. BUT you will have enough useless facts and confusing theories to keep your English teacher occupied for a whole term - that way, you can avoid doing real English lessons at all and get your English teacher sacked when the whole class fails their next exam - that'll teach them!

GOBBLE-DE-GOOK

English is probably the silliest language in the world so here are some useful facts to help you survive it...

Since 'i' always goes before 'e' except after 'c', you can ignore words like leisure and rein because they don't exist.

Substitute 'f' for 'ph' to make things easier when spelling words like FOTOGRAF, FYSICS, GEOGRAFY AND EMFASIS.

Since 'rough' is pronounced 'ruff' and 'through' pronounced 'threw', ignore the proper spelling and write your homework in plain English. For example:

THE RUFF BOY COFFED SO HARD THAT THE TEECHER'S HED FELL OFF AND EVERYONE LAFFED THREW THE LESSEN!

You may wonder why words like 'there' and 'their' or 'place' and 'plaice' sound the same but mean something completely different? Well, don't. It's not your problem if teachers can't make their minds up and if they ask you to sit in a different plaice just tell them not to be cruel to flatfish - that should confuse them!

....and Comprehension, which basically means 'have you understood what you have just read?' - **the correct answer is No.**

You will be forced to study punctuation - learn these off by heart:

, ; ' "
? !!!

Finally, there's English Literature which means poetry, plays and novels - most of these are not written by English people at all but by Scots, Irish, Welsh and Americans - what a con!

DOUBLE DUTCH

Question: How many words in the English language are English?

Answer: Hardly any!

Here are some examples:

• **TEA** comes from the Dutch who stole it from the Chinese even though we've been drinking it ever since.

• **TEACH** is German.

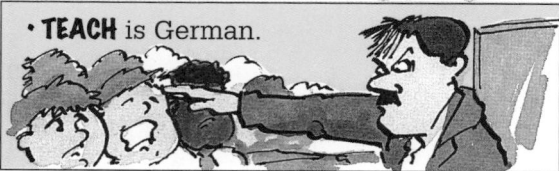

• **ALPHABET** comes from the Greeks.

• **SCHOOL** began life as the Greek word 'skhole', was kidnapped by the Romans and became 'scola' then ended up in France as 'école' before we hijacked it - pity they didn't leave it where it was and save us a lot of trouble!

- **CORRIDOR** is Italian
- **DESK** is Latin
- **PENCIL** is French
- **BAG** is Norse (as in Vikings) and ...
- **TANDOORI TAKE AWAY** is definitely Indian!

Even English names aren't safe - take a famous Englishman like Admiral Horatio Nelson.

Admiral comes from an Arabic word for 'commander'. Horatio comes from Latin and means 'keeper of the hours'. Nelson comes from 'son of Helene' from a French word meaning 'light'; all of which means our most famous admiral should be called 'the light commander of the clock'. Look up your own name in a babies' names book to see what you should be called.

(I hope it isn't Cecil – that means 'blind one' in Latin!)

WANNABEES

**English teachers are a dangerous lot -
if they don't bore you to death reading
endless streams of poetry (See page 12),
they will probably embarrass you to
death by insisting that you play a part
in the school play (See page 42).**

That's because all English teachers are
frustrated poets, playwrights, actors and
novelists who would much rather be doing
any of these things than teaching a crowd
of spotty little *oiks* who don't know their Ps
from their Qs and think William
Wordsworth played centre forward
for Millwall in 1988.

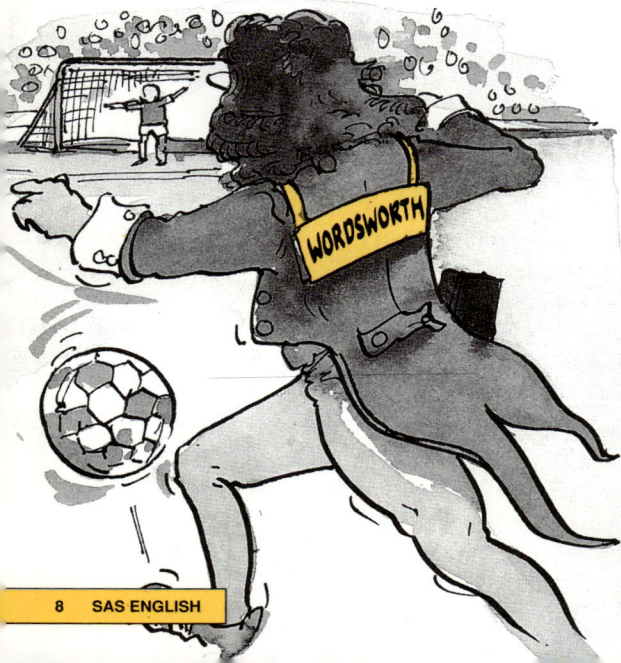

When they ask you what you wannabee when you grow up, do not say a doctor, a scientist or a centre forward for Millwall - your English teacher will make your life miserable; the right answer is...

"I wannabee an actor with the Royal Shakespeare Company or I wannabee a famous poet."

Your English teacher will then love you and give you top marks in all their tests - even if you can't spell your own name.

Of course, if your own name is Bartamaeus MacSwithinbotham, that would be perfectly understandable.

USELESS EUSTACE

Here are some useless facts about English which were collected by Eustace Von Idiot in his entertaining volume, The Rise and Fall of the Dodo. Use them to distract your teacher so they forget to give you homework...

Among the longest words in the English language are:

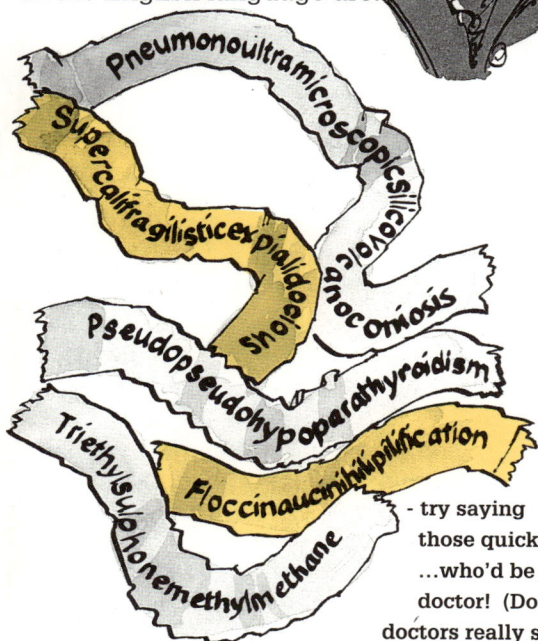

Pneumonoultramicroscopicsilicovolcanoconiosis

Supercalifragilisticexpialidocious

Pseudopseudohypoparathyroidism

Floccinaucinihilipilification

Triethylsulphonemethylmethane

- try saying those quickly ...who'd be a doctor! (Do doctors really say Supercalifragilisticexpialidocious?)

The most expensive English book in the world is:

The Gospels of Henry the Lion published around 1173-75 which sold at auction in Sotheby's, London, on 6th December, 1983, for a cool £7,400,000 - and that's more pocket money than you earn in a fortnight!

The cheapest English book in the world is:

Your homework jotter, which isn't worth anything because it's full of the most pathetic rubbish ever written...and when your dad finds out, you probably won't earn any more pocket money ever and will have to leave school at the age of fourteen and take up a career as a leaf sweeper in the New Forest - you have been warned!

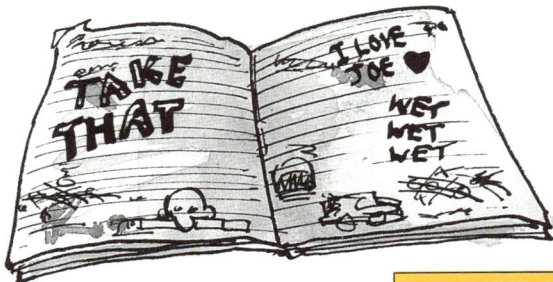

POTTY POETS

**All poets are potty - so would *you* be if you spent all your time trying to make the ends of your sentences rhyme.
Of course, some people are poets even though they don't know it!**

Here are some famous lines from some famous poets to impress your teacher with:

> I wandered lonely as a cloud
> That floats on high o'er vales and hills,
> When all at once I saw a crowd
> Of Americans waving dollar bills...
> *The Tourist Trade*, after a poem by
> William Wordsworth.

The Assyrian came down
Like the wolf on the fold
And his cohorts were gleaming
In purple and gold
And the sheen of their spears
Was like stars on the sea
But they'd missed the last bus
And were late home for tea...
Public Transport, after a
poem by Lord Byron.

The Oak is called the King of Trees,
The Aspen quivers in the breeze,
The Poplar grows up straight and tall,
Until the axeman fells them all...
  and turns them into matches.

A Short History of the Safety Match,
after a poem by Samuel Coleridge,

Oh, to be in England
Now that April's there.
And whoever wakes in England
Sees the rain still pouring there.

Springtime, after a poem by Robert Browning,

Oh, young Lochinvar is come out
of the West,
Through all the wide Border his
steed was the best,
And save his good broadsword he
weapons had none
His chance of survival was 90-1.

The Stupid Soldier, after a poem by Sir Walter Scott

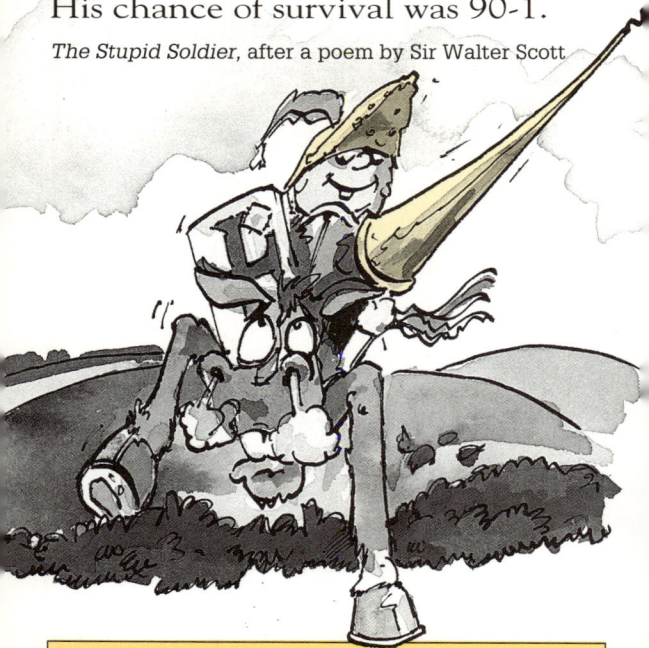

Below the thunders of the upper deep;
Far, far beneath in the abysmal sea,
His ancient, dreamless, uninvaded sleep -
Snored the teacher of RE...
A Portrait of the Staffroom,
after a poem by Alfred, Lord Tennyson

If you can keep your head when
all about you

Are losing theirs and blaming it
on you;

If you can trust yourself when all
men doubt you,

But make allowance for their
doubting too;

If you can wait and not be tired
by waiting,

Or being lied about, don't deal
in lies,

If you can smile, although
frustrating,

When the burger bar runs out
of fries…

If It Happens Again, after a poem
by Rudyard Kipling

THE BARD

This is the name given to our most famous playwright, Mr William Shakespeare (known as Billy Boy to his friends).

He should really be called 'The Bored' because that's what you will be once you have suffered one of his plays.

For a start, poor old Shakespeare is not very up-to-date and his plays are full of 'thee's' and 'thou's' and 'dost's' and 'doest's' that nobody would be seen dead using today - of course, he is dead so that might explain it!

If your English teacher asks for volunteers to act in a Shakespeare play, dive under your desk and pretend to be a discarded lump of chewing gum until some other idiots have put their hands up - you do not want to take part because all Shakespeare's characters are either murdered, driven insane, chopped into pieces or turned into animals by evil fairies.

In Shakespeare's day the audience was allowed to boo the actors, throw rotten tomatoes onto the stage and generally have a good time - so you might suggest this to your teacher for the next school production. At least it would be more fun than watching some twit in tights talking to a skull which he thinks is his best friend Yoric.

IDIOT'S GUIDE

Here is a quick guide to some of Shakespeare's best known plays to impress your teacher with:

Hamlet - a tragedy about three little pigs who have their house blown down and are turned into Danish bacon.

Macbeth - an everyday tale about three witches trying to invent a new kind of soup which is to be called Macbeth's Original Eye of Newt and Toe of Frog Broth - it is not a success!

The Taming of the Shrew - an amusing story about a clever shrew called Katharina who runs away to join the circus.

Romeo and Juliet - a revolting story where these two horribly handsome people meet through a lonely hearts dating agency and actually fall in love - hard to believe, isn't it?

Measure for Measure -
a school's educational play about the lesser
known units of the metric system.

The Merry Wives of Windsor
- concerns a syndicate of
women who win an early
version of the National
Lottery and try to buy
Windsor Castle from
the Queen.

Julius Caesar - this is a spelling mistake as
the original title was Julius - Seize Her!
It is about this Roman bloke who goes
chasing after the Queen of Egypt on a
cruise up the Nile.

The Comedy of Errors - the original title of this
play has long been forgotten - the actors
were under-rehearsed on the first night,
and had to make it up as they went along.
The audience thought it was an hilarious
comedy - shame it was supposed to be a
serious drama!

BORING NIGHT OUT

One of the greatest dangers you will have to face whilst being taught English is being taken for a trip to the theatre. The evening will go something like this:

1 Packed into school bus like sardines in a fish factory.

2 Driven to theatre by unqualified temporary stand-in driver who thinks he's Damon Hill.

3 Lined up outside theatre like prisoners in a chain gang.

4 Lectured by teacher on behaviour, manners, etc.

"Right, you lot, this is a brilliantly funny play and you are privileged to see it. Anyone found laughing will be thrown out. Do not shout at the actors or throw rotten tomatoes and NO talking!"

5 Frisked for chewing gum, sweet wrappers, crisps, rotten tomatoes, catapults, whoopie cushions and anything else that might cause a noise.

6 Ordered to your seats - this takes hours and involves a lot of chopping and changing in case anyone is sitting beside their best friend as this is not allowed in case you accidentally enjoy yourself. You will be seated behind a seven feet tall gorilla with a haystack on his head, and will not see the play anyway.

7 The play begins but the actors are struck by chronic stage fright at the sight of your ugly faces and forget their lines.

8 The curtain goes down early and a riot breaks out.

9 You all go home and ten people are sick on the bus, three of them down the back of your neck.

And a lovely time was had by all!

LIBRARY LOBOTOMY

Here is a good trick for driving the school librarian crazy.

Order one of the following from Eustace Von Idiot's Guide To Non-Bestsellers; (I promise you they are all real books but the librarian will never be able to track them down):

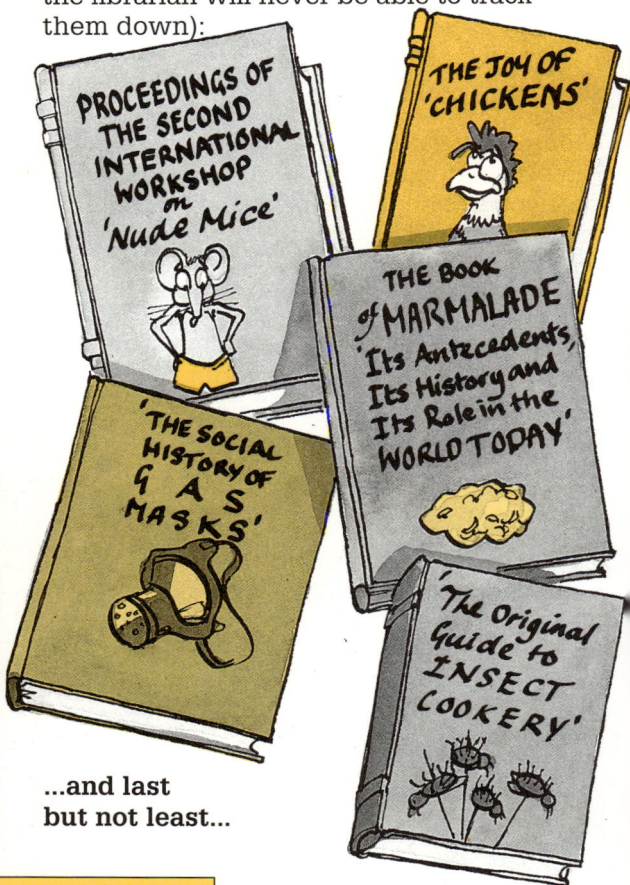

PROCEEDINGS OF THE SECOND INTERNATIONAL WORKSHOP on 'Nude Mice'

THE JOY OF 'CHICKENS'

THE BOOK of MARMALADE 'Its Antecedents, Its History and Its Role in the WORLD TODAY'

'THE SOCIAL HISTORY OF GAS MASKS'

'The Original Guide to INSECT COOKERY'

...and last but not least...

When the librarian can't find any of them, you could always hunt in one of the bigger libraries in the UK:

Name	Location	Date	No. of books
British Library	London	1753	18,000,000
Bodleian Library	Oxford	1602	5,000,000
National Library of Scotland	Edinburgh	1682	5,000,000
University of Cambridge	Cambridge	c1400	5,000,000
Lancashire County Library	Preston	1924	3,560,000

So you've no excuse - there's always a good book you haven't read yet!

NUMBSKULLS

Yes, your skull will be numb once you've read the novels on your reading list.

The books you have to read are called 'classics'. This is because they have six classes to fulfil before they qualify. The six classes are:

Age The book must be very old and preferably written in Ye Olde Style English so it is doubly difficult to read.

Content With the odd exception, like *Treasure Island* (which is actually quite exciting in places and shouldn't be on the list), the main story of the book must be extremely boring. A good example is *Little Women* which is about a tribe of pygmies who talk a lot.

Readership Classics are only read for enjoyment by people over the age of sixty-five, and English teachers.

Title All classics should have really weird titles like *Wuthering Heights* or *Martin Chuzzlewit.*

Length It is important that the book is virtually endless and has at least two hundred chapters.

Weight All classics are so heavy that you need a specially strengthened school bag and a team of porters to carry them home.

EASY PEASY

Learn these quick revision notes on some famous novels:

Jane Eyre by Charlotte Brontesaurus – a miserable story about a little orphan girl who should have been horse-whipped and deported to Australia but ends up instead in a mansion in Yorkshire - big deal.

Oliver Twist by Charles What-the-Dickens - a miserable story about a little orphan boy who should have been horse-whipped and deported to Australia but ends up meeting a really nice man called Fagan instead.

Kidnapped by Robert Loopy Stephenson – a ripping yarn about a baby goat falling asleep in the Highlands of Scotland.

The Rover by Joseph Conrod – another ripping yarn about a big dog searching for his favourite bone.

Animal Farm by George Unwell – a famous story about a mutiny of battery reared chickens who stuff the farmer into a tiny cage and make him eat rubbish - not for the squeamish.

Lord of the Flies by William Moulding – a chilling horror story about a swarm of killer bluebottles.

A Tale of Two Cities also by Charles What-the-Dickens - a very limited series of travel guides.

Huckleberry Finn by Mark Twerp – the adventures of a goldfish lost in the Mississippi River.

FAT FACTS

Some more useless facts from Eustace
Von Idiot to bore your teacher with...

BESTSELLING CLASSICS:

1 *Wuthering Heights* by Emily Brontë
2 *Hard Times* by Charles Dickens
3 *Pride and Prejudice* by Jane Austen
4 *Jane Eyre* by Charlotte Brontë
5 *Great Expectations* by
   Charles Dickens

BESTSELLING COMICS:

1 The Beano (1938 -)
2 Comic Cuts (1890-1953)
3 The Dandy (1937 -)
4 The Eagle (1941-1969)
5 Film Fun (1890-1953)

WORDS WITH THE MOST MEANINGS IN THE OXFORD ENGLISH DICTIONARY:

1. Set (464)
2. Run (396)
3. Go (368)
4. Take (343)
5. Stand (334)

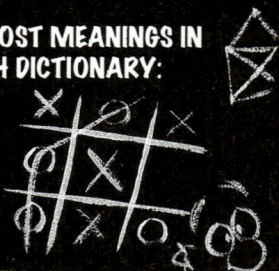

THE MOST TRANSLATED AUTHORS IN THE WORLD:

1. V. I. Lenin
2. Agatha Christie
3. Jules Verne
4. William Shakespeare
5. Enid Blyton

....and finally, Shakespeare's longest play is Hamlet which has 3,901 lines. Some people think he should have been given 3,901 lines by his English teacher - 'I must not write any more plays'.

I SAY, I SAY, I SAY

Here are some well known sayings and phrases that will be most useful for your English studies:

A stitch in grime saves time - by Professor I. M. Bloodthirsty, chief surgeon at the Royal Hospital for Unnecessary Operations.

Too many rooks spoil the broth - by the author of Four and Twenty Blackbirds Baked in a Pie.

More haste, less speed - by George Snail, inventor of the portable house.

People in glass houses shouldn't throw gnomes - by the Chief Gnome, Sir Aardvark Clutterbuck, OBE.

The cow jumped over the moon - by I. M. A. Lunatic who needs his eyes tested.

Who bares wins - motto of the Sunny Shade nudist colony's formation dancing team.

A friend in need is best avoided - from Mr A. Meanie, Director of the Institute of International Banking.

He who laughs last gets tummy ache - Nurse B. Grim, chairperson of the Let's Be Miserable Foundation.

Children should be clean and not haired - motto of the Keep Children Bald campaign.

There's no business like woebusiness - from the Funeral Director's Guild.

One man's wheat is another man's poison - last words of a cereal killer.

Honour fly father and fly mother - from the Bluebottle Family Guidance Council.

As sick as a carrot - what poorly vegetarians say.

GRIM GRAMMAR

Learning English involves, amongst other things, trying to remember the difference between verbs, adverbs, nouns, pronouns, adjectives and all those other little words that you can't remember the difference between.

Here is a study aid to help you. Just pick the most suitable words in the brackets to complete the following...

I (slithered, hopped, crawled) along the (canal, race track, escalator) on my way to (school, prison, China). With me were my pet (gorilla, goldfish, rubber plant) and my little sister who is called (Bathsheba, Appendicitis, Gangrene).

It was the first day of the new term and we were looking forward to (eating, beating, meeting) our new teacher, Mrs Longshortly, who was famous for her (bungee jumping, talons, talents) and taught (karate, English, karaoke) at my new school (Bash Street, Custard Pie, Hell's Kitchen) Comprehensive.

"Good morning, little (monsters, vermin, creeps)," said Mrs Longshortly once we had all sat down in our (pyjamas, leotards, electric chairs).

"I am so (disgusted, horrified, terrified) to meet you all. Today we are going to learn all about (Attila the Hun, Ghenghis Khan, Winnie the Pooh) for our domestic science project. As you know he was a great (chef, janitor, Head Master) of this school in days gone by. Now please get out your exercise (machines, blotters, yards) and take down the following (notes, goats, boats)."

The lesson went quickly and everyone enjoyed themselves picking their (projects, noses, daffodils).

Then it was breaktime. I ate some of my (wild buffalo, snake, toad) sandwiches and washed them down with a (barrel, lake, slop bucket) of orange juice.

After break it was time for English with Mr (Shakespeare, Rasputin, Mole) who was going to teach us all about (flower arranging, torture, motor mechanics) for beginners.

Unfortunately, just as he was about to start, the school was attacked by a rampaging group of (dinosaurs, inspectors, soldier ants). Several teachers and pupils were (dissolved in acid, crushed to a pulp, eaten alive) and the rest of us had to be sent home early.

Still, all in all, this was a most interesting start to my new school career and I can hardly wait until tomorrow.

So, can you now claim you know a verb from any other stupid part of the language? Thought not. But you could always look them up in a boring book, if you're really THAT interested...

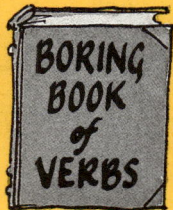

BORING BOOK of VERBS

EXCUSES, EXCUSES

English teachers are great ones for giving extra marks for imagination and creativity, so they should appreciate some of your reasons for being late for their class:

- The school bus got to the bus stop before I did.

- The bus was hijacked and the hijackers made the bus driver fly to Rome.

- My paper round blew away and it took me an hour to catch it.

- I helped an old lady across the road, but it took longer than I expected because she didn't want to go.

- The sign down the road said, "School - Go Slow", so I dutifully obeyed it.

- I was dreaming about a football match, and it went into extra time.

- I was running so fast to get to school on time that when I got to the gates I couldn't stop.

- My alarm clock had a lie in.

- I got up, got dressed, had my breakfast and came to school. When I got here I found it was just a dream, so I had to go all the way home to wake myself up and then get dressed, have my breakfast and come to school.

From time to time you will be given a piece of writing by your English teacher who will ask you to read it, then answer questions to show if you have understood it - this is called Comprehension.

You might as well practise this boring task by reading the following story then answering the questions on page 39.

The Giant Slug

Once upon a time a nutty professor, Cashew N. Walnut, invented the Extra-Large Laser Blast Kit machine that could enlarge anything to two hundred times its normal size.

He used it to enlarge cabbages, cauliflowers, carrots and cucumbers so that no one in the world need ever be hungry again.

Unfortunately, he did not check his cabbages carefully enough and one day something huge, squishy and incredibly bad-tempered crawled out of a leaf the size of Wembley Stadium.

"Look out!" his assistant, Ebeneezer Sneezer, shouted as the giant mollusc crawled towards them.

It was too late; the professor was quickly swamped by an avalanche of slug slime and Ebeneezer just managed to escape by jumping on to the back of a hippopotamus that happened to be passing by.

The giant slug roamed the earth causing death and destruction wherever it went. It ate the tropical rainforests for breakfast, the American prairie for lunch and would have finished off with the Canadian backwoods for dessert if Ebeneezer had not arrived in the nick of time with seventeen tonnes of best sea salt.

This was sprinkled on the slug from a fleet of helicopters. . .

Writing in agony, the giant slug dissolved there and then causing major flooding in six states of America. The President of the U.S.A. announced a state of emergency and the National Guard were ordered in with mops and buckets to clear up the mess.

But the world had been saved from a fate worse than death, by Ebeneezer, who destroyed the Extra-Large Laser Blast Kit to prevent any more accidents.

Everybody would have lived happily ever after... if it wasn't for the spider which had also been lurking in that ill-fated cabbage...

QUESTION TIME

Now you have read The Giant Slug, **answer the following questions.**

1 Why was the professor called Cashew N. Walnut?

2 What size is two hundred times normal?

3 Why was the leaf the size of Wembley Stadium?

4 Why was the professor's assistant called Ebeneezer?

5 What do you call a passing hippopotamus?

6 Why was the slug going to eat the backwoods for dessert?

7 Where did Ebeneezer get his salt?

8 In the story, what does U.S.A. stand for?

9 What is a fate worse than death?

10 What do you think the moral of the story is?

Answers:

1 Because he was nutty.

2 Very big.

3 Because it was bigger than Anfield

4 Because that was his name.

5 A hippo passing us.

6 Because it was too big to trifle with.

7 From a salt seller.

8 Undesirable Slugs Agency.

9 Two periods of English on the same day.

10 Never put all your slugs in one Blast Kit.

MORE POTTY POEMS

Another collection of famous lines from famous poets.

The sun descending in the west,
The evening star does shine,
The birds are silent in their nest,
'Cause I just shot one hundred and nine...

    By William Flake, from his poem
    Hunting Sparrows with a Shotgun

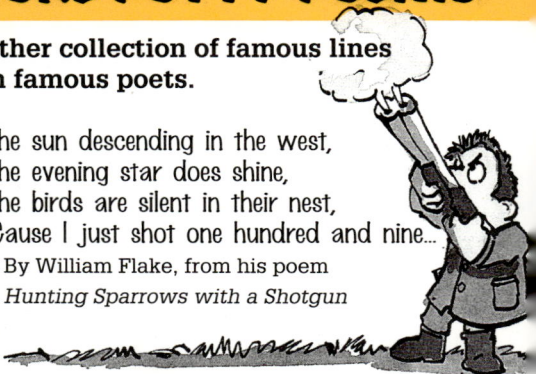

At the door on summer evenings
Sat the little Hiawatha;
Heard the whispering of the pine trees,
Just before the beastie got her...

    By Henry Wadsworth Shortfellow,
    from his poem *The Good, The Bad and the Great
    Big Hairy Thing From Another Planet*

The Owl and the Pussy-cat went to sea
In a beautiful pea-green boat.
It sank like a stone, they'd no right to moan,
They forgot to find out, would it float?

    By Edward Beer, from his poem *Safety At Sea*

On the grassy banks
Lambkins at their pranks;
Woolly sisters, woolly brothers,
Jumping off their feet
Until the jolly butchers
Turn them into meat...

By Christina Spaghetti, from her poem
Not for Vegetarians

Someone came knocking
At my wee, small door;
Someone came knocking,
I'm sure-sure-sure;
I listened, I opened,
I looked to left and right,
But I didn't see it coming
'Til it gave me such a bite.

By Walter De La Pear, from his poem
The Thing That Went Chomp In The Night

FOOL'S PLAY

Once a year (or more if you're unlucky) you will have to learn to survive the school play. This is the ritual where parents and friends are dragged in off the street and forced to sit through at least one, probably two hours of pure torture.

You have to take part. There is no escape;
- Drama teachers are merciless in hunting down 'volunteers';
- Art teachers collar anyone who can hold a paintbrush;
- Music teachers don't care whether you can actually play an instrument as long as you can hold one to fill out the orchestra;
- English teachers will spend months telling you how wonderful the play is and how much you are going to enjoy yourself - **DO NOT BE TAKEN IN.**

School plays are more boring than watching the tide come in and the only way you are going to enjoy yourself is by breaking a leg and spending the time in hospital. Incidentally, breaking a leg might not be so difficult to achieve...it is considered bad luck to wish any actor **"Good Luck"** before a performance - **"Break a leg"** is actual theatre-lovey-speak! So, if you **DO** happen to dance over-enthusiastically off the stage in the dress rehearsal, then you were only following the instructions, quite literally...

The best advice is to volunteer to help with make-up or lighting - that way you can at least avoid making a fool of yourself on the stage or having to help paint unlimited acres of scenery. Alternatively, you could volunteer to be the back end of a stage horse. It might not sound like fun, but it's more fun than ending up in the part of Romeo and having to wear tights.

HELP!

In case you still think the play might be fun, please read the following carefully and remember - the school play can seriously damage your health.

Facts about school plays - what you need to know:

1 You will have to sing on your own, at the front of the stage, with a great big spotlight shining in your face.

2 All your friends in the audience will laugh at you and pull funny faces to put you off.

3 You will have to wear a ridiculous costume that doesn't fit properly and smells as though a family of mice have been nesting in it - which they probably have.

4 When you forget your lines, some wretched person in the wings will 'whisper' them to prompt you. However, this could be the drama teacher, and the prompt will be a stage whisper, audible to the audience and any passing motorists outside. NOW try and pretend you didn't fluff your lines.

5 The make-up you have to wear will make spots burst out all over your skin like miniature volcanoes.

6 You will undoubtedly be cast in the leading 'romantic-sap' role and will have to kiss the school geek.

7 Your parents will hate you because they will feel obliged to come to the play even though they've always avoided it before and would much prefer to sit at home watching television. Don't feel guilty - make them suffer with you.

8 Beware of over-enthusiastic parents (yours or anybody else's) with video cameras. Enough said…

9 If you are in an all boys' school, you will have to dress up as a girl.

10 If you are in an all girls' school, you will have to dress up as a boy.

…but remember - if you don't take part in the play, everyone will call you a 'wet blanket' or a 'party pooper' and no one will ever be your friend again - so you can't win, no matter what you do!

SCHOOL LIBRARY

So, your librarian has recovered from your last visit? Challenge them to find these books in their archives - and if they haven't got a copy, then you're terribly sorry, you just can't do your homework, and it's all their fault...

RAISING THE WIND by Tina Beans

ROAD TRANSPORT by Laurie Driver

STOP SWEARING! by A Pauline Langwidge

Learning to Ride a Horse by MAJOR BUMSORE

Seasons Greetings by Mary Krissmas

Old Furniture by ANN TIQUE

IS IT YOURS? BY JOAN ITT

CAR REPAIRS by MIKE ANNICK

STICK 'EM UP BY BILL POSTER

Pamper your CHILDREN by Molly Coddle